Residential Landscape Design for the Horticulturally Hopeless

by Mike Dooley

First published by Dog Ear Publishing
4010 W. 86th Street, Ste H
Indianapolis, IN 46268
www.dogearpublishing.net

ISBN: 978-145750-235-4

This book is printed on acid-free paper.

Printed in the United States of America

Acknowledgments

A big "thank you" to Mike Foley for being a great and patient friend, and creating the Horticulturally Hopeless character.

I would also like to thank Jennifer Huard for her help and support with the manuscript, book cover and website-you're the best.

Much thanks to Ben, Michelle, Cerina and Angel, you've always believed in me-I love you all.

Special thanks to Leslie my friend, my supporter and my partner.

Finally, a great big thanks to Abbey the Dog for not barking while I wrote this book.

Table of Contents

Introduction

This is not a book on landscape plants. This book shows you how to design with landscape plants. There are books available on the subject of "landscape design" and they'll give you some basic guidelines and show you beautiful photos of landscapes that most of us could never afford and certainly could not install ourselves.

To my knowledge this is the only book available that shows the average homeowner or budding designer a step-by-step approach to developing simple yet practical ideas and put them on paper in a usable way.

I'm not going to show you fancy graphic techniques that you don't need and you won't be asked to buy a drafting board or software. I will show you how to draw a simple plan and stay within budget.

When completed, you'll have a "to scale" plan ready to install yourself or to put out for bids. If you're a new landscape professional without the design skills that you need to succeed, then I think this book will be of great help.

Happy Gardening

Mike Dooley

How to Use This Book

This is a very unique book and requires special instructions for its use.

First, you'll need a local information source to make a list of plants that do well in your area. This is easy to obtain on the internet, from the local Master Gardeners or through plant books written specifically for your area. Western Garden book list 32 climate zones in the western United States alone and many of these zones have their own special plants. To provide you with all of the local plant information needed for each climate zone in United States would require many volumes and only serve to confuse the reader. This is why I don't make plant selections for you and your special climate zone.

The reason that a landscape design book like this has not been attempted previously is that overcoming this problem requires a unique design technique that can be easily adapted for these local plants. I've developed a simple technique that gets around this problem and it's explained in detail in chapter 4.

The key to success in laying out the hardscape is learning to adapt the sample plans to your special situation. This information is found in chapter 3.

Finally, deciding where to put the plants on your revised sample plan is a matter of "plugging them in" based primarily on their height, width and shade tolerance. More creative people may want to use the plans as guidelines only and create on their own. Chapter 4 gives you the directions that you'll need to work thru the plant placement.

1

Getting Started

What Do I Need?

The following is a list of what you'll need for the project. Some of the items you already have and some can be borrowed. A few of the items can be substituted and others will need to be purchased.

- Tape measure at least 20'
- Graph paper 8x11 with one quarter inch squares.
- Number 2 pencils
- Eraser
- Paper for the enlarged design

Standard drafting paper without a grid is easy to draw on and especially easy to copy. Or, you can tape together the 8.5"x11"gragh paper to make a larger sheet if you don't want to buy drafting paper. Twenty four inch wide drafting paper with a one quarter inch grid is great and will make life much easier. Before you decide what kind of paper to buy refer to "Measuring and Layout" below. You need to decide if you want to count squares to get your measurements on paper or if you want to use the architect's scale to draw with. Most new designers like to just count the squares on a sheet of drafting paper that is large enough for the entire project. Read the section on "Enlarging the Sketch without a Survey" before buying paper.

- Ruler or an architect's scale to make it easier (architect scales only cost 3 or 4 dollars and keep you from doing calculation every time you measure). Do not buy an engineer's scale, they are different.
- Tracing paper is very handy
- A circle template is needed or even better is a compass that will make any size circle that you may need.

Optional Items

- Colored pencils if you want to color your plan. This will make it easier to organize the bloom colors of the plants.
- A triangle to keep the corners square as you draw. Any square object like a book will work in a pinch.
- A clip board to hold graft paper

-Information for your plant list

You will need a good book on plants for your specific area. A book on desert plants, western plants or plants of the east coast will not work! General books on xeric plants, native plants or herbs will not work either. You will want a regional book with color photos about the plants that grow in your city or at the very least your region. The book you pick must have a list of plants for your specific area or you're wasting your money and time. For local advice on the book to buy, call your local agricultural extension office and ask for the horticultural department or better yet call the Master Gardeners in your area. With a little luck they'll have produced a website with the list you will need and you won't need to buy a book.

Sometimes a local landscape contractor or nursery will have a website that will show you the best plants for your area. If you just go to the nursery and make a list of plants that you like you'll not get the information you need to produce your plan. When you see a plant in a nursery it's a snap shot of the plant, and if it has poor or limited signage you don't get the information you need. Nursery signage is designed to sell plants and not designed to tell you some of the plant characteristics that are more negative; like insect problems or allergy concerns.

If you' re going to do your own hardscape or irrigation, a good detailed book on the subject will be of great help or you can search

YouTube videos for free. Call around and some of the local irrigation wholesaler/retailers may draw an irrigation plan for free if you buy all the parts from them. They'll be a great source for troubleshooting when you need it. This is a good place to make a friend. Irrigation contractors will usually draw you a plan for a fee. Just because your spouse can repair a leaky faucet doesn't mean that he or she can install a sprinkler system that works well.

Measuring and Layout
Scale

Let's spend a moment talking about scale so we can determine what size paper we need. If you purchased an architect's scale you'll notice different scales as you rotate it. To conserve space (and to drive you crazy) the manufacturer put two scales on each side. One reads from left to right and the other reads from right to left. Flip the scale over until it reads one quarter. This is the scale that is probably right for most home owners unless you have a huge property. If you do have a really large property then you may have to switch to one eighth scale.

What does scale mean? It's really simple; one quarter inch scale means that one quarter inch on the plan equals 1 foot on the ground. The quarter inch scale is just dividing itself into the quarter inches that you need and then numbering them for your convenience. If you use a ruler instead of a scale, then when you measure 6 inches on the ruler you must multiply it by four to know that it is really 24 feet. If you accidentally switch scales in the middle of your project, you'll have big problems. One way to prevent this is to put masking tape over all the other scales so you can't accidentally use them.

Without a Survey

Measuring is the first step in our process and can be very easy if you have a rectangular lot with a rectangular house. On the other hand, if you have many angles or curved property lines it will be more challenging. It's usually easier to put the back yard on a separate page from the front yard if you'll be designing both. This will make it easier for two reasons. First you don't need as large a surface to draw on and second, in the installation phase, you'll not be carrying around a huge piece of paper as you lay it out.

Get a clip board and a pad of paper with one-quarter inch squares, the paper should be at least eight and one half by eleven inches. If your area is larger than 44 feet x 34 feet and you start counting squares to equal one foot, your property will not fit on an 8 ½" x 11" paper. If it won't fit on the paper, don't count squares; just use the grid to help draw straight lines. The grid on the paper will still make it much easier to draw the property and keep things looking proportional.

Go stand at the property line, draw the area as best you can, it doesn't have to be in perfect proportion because we're going to use your measurements not the drawing to make the enlargement.

After you have the property drawn, it's time to measure. Start at one corner of the house and measure along the walls. Write down the measurements along the appropriate lines on your sketch and continue until the house measurements are done. The house is the easiest to draw because it's almost always a series of ninety degree angles. The problems arise with the property lines that are not ninety degree angles or worse yet, not even straight lines. See the diagram "Measuring the Property". Sight along a wall of the house and measure to the property lines and/or fences. Write down the measurements to the fences or property lines. Look at the diagram and this will make sense. Use this method to plot the location of all the shrubs, trees and hardscape that will remain (if you are doing a makeover of an existing landscape.) Now, we have the sketch done and we are ready to enlarge it.

Enlarging the Sketch WITHOUT a Survey

Now that you know something about scale, we're ready to enlarge the plan to a size that we can work with. The plan must be drawn "to scale" so that you can accurately space the plants and measure the grass, gravel or bark that you need for the project.

I know what you're thinking. You think "close is good enough." If you don't draw "to scale" think of how costly and irritating it will be to blindly order plants and truckloads of materials when you don't know how much you need. Please go to the effort to transfer the measurements and draw it to quarter inch scale.

Here is how you do it: Get out your sketch and add up the width of the property. Do the same thing with the depth. Let's say the yard measures 80 feet across by 40 feet deep. Using your scale or ruler, measure 80 feet of width and 40 feet of depth on your table and you'll see the size that the project will take up on your paper. Paper that is 24 inches top to bottom can hold a yard that is almost 96 feet deep. You need a little margin here so, 90 feet would probably be the maximum width that would fit. If you bought paper on a roll it doesn't really matter how wide the property is because it'll fit. If you're buying cut sheets of paper this process will tell you how wide the paper must be that you purchase. So, now we have the sketch and the paper and we're ready to start.

You know how large the overall project is going to be on the paper so judge how close a corner must be to the edge and start drawing at that corner. This'll work well if you have a lot with squared corners and straight property lines. If you have curved property lines and corners that are not square then it is much easier to draw the house in the middle of the paper and then add the property lines around it. What usually happens when things go wrong is that you're drawing around the yard in a circular fashion and when you get back to where the lines should meet

...they don't. Oh my, now we have a problem. Don't worry; it happens to the pros all the time. There are only a couple of things that can be wrong.

First, using your scale or ruler, check to see if every line is the same length as the number you wrote on the sketch. (This is where you wish that you'd bought that scale.) If that doesn't solve the problem, step outside and take a close look at the property while looking at the sketch and see if you missed a wall or other measurement. If that doesn't solve the problem, then you measured wrong and the number that you wrote down on the sketch is incorrect.

The part that is a little tough is the curved property lines. (Refer back to "Measuring" diagram and this description will make sense) Think of the house that you have already drawn as a separate object. If you sighted along the walls of the house and took the measurements to the property line in several places, then using your scale, transfer the measurements to the paper and make dots where the property lines or fences should be. Now, connect the dots and you have the perimeter drawn around the house. At this point, if you're measuring a large lot with curved property lines and you're within a couple of feet, then you may say "that's good enough". Check all your measurement to be sure. Now you're ready to draw in the hardscape.

Tip: Hardscape is a term for all the concrete and masonry.

Enlarging the Sketch WITH a Survey

Most of the measuring can be avoided if you have a survey with your house papers. They're required on all home loans, so if you didn't pay cash for the house then you have one. Get your survey and don't enlarge it or reduce it yourself! After you have the survey, you still must use the above explanation to draw in all the hardscape to scale (like added side-walks and patios) that was not present when the survey was made. You'll then add in all the plants or trees that you want to keep if you are doing a makeover of an existing landscape. Now, we can start the enlargement process.

Take your survey to a reprographics print shop and tell them to enlarge it to one quarter inch scale. If you just go to the local copy shop this throws them a curve for some reason. If you go to a reprographics shop, they'll know what you are trying to do and you just saved a lot of time and stress!

Always check that the reprographics shop did the enlargement cor-rectly. To do this simply use the scale or a ruler and confirm the mea-surements on the enlarged plan. Also, check any hardscape that was done after the survey and any existing plants to remain and make sure you have them in the right place.

Please do not use a "site plan" unless you confirm that it's accurate. Surveys are made after the house was built and are normally accurate. Site plans show what the builder wanted to build not what they actually built. Now, we have the survey enlarged and all the features added that were installed after the survey was done and will remain. Now we're ready to design.

2

Basic Design Considerations

Let's Be Real
Style
Plant Maintenance and Turf Grass
Computer Aided Design (CAD)
Oversized Lots

Let's Be Real

This is where we start to put our "wish list" together and we must be very honest with ourselves concerning what we really want, how much hard work we will be willing to do and what we can afford.

As a professional designer, I very often have to get people to snap back into reality at this point. This is not HGTV. You will very likely be doing the work or at the very least be paying someone to do it for you.

Let's say that you have an average back yard and it is sixty-foot-by-forty-foot. Let's assume that you want it to look very nice but you can't get carried away spending money and time. The average back yard that I install will cost you three or four dollars per square foot without any hardscape. With twenty-four hundred square foot to install, you are looking at around eighty-four hundred dollars to have the project done for you.

The average landscape installer can install about seven hundred dollars a day in retail prices. In this case, it would take one man (in his twenties) twelve days to do the project. We will assume that you are not in your twenties so you would be lucky to do five hundred dollars a day. Now your project will take one person seventeen days to complete or a couple of months working every weekend! The good news is that you will save around four thousand dollars in the process and have bragging rights that are well deserved.

Before you take the book to the trash can, let's consider a couple of things. First, you can get a friend or spouse to help and really cut down the time. Secondly, you could have a local landscaper do the really hard parts and you could do the easier parts of the project. None of this estimated pricing includes patios, retaining walls or gazebos! These estimates are for grass, edger, mulch, gravel, plants and maybe irrigation.

Knowing this, you may want to rethink the tennis court and swimming pool. Make a list of what you're willing to install, what you could have installed and what you can live without. Some of the things that you "must have" can be rethought.

Here is an example of a couple of the situations that arise. Many of my clients say they want a vegetable garden. My usual response is the following series of questions: Have you ever grown a garden before? Do you usually like yard work? Do you eat a lot of vegetables or do you just like fresh tomatoes? First let me say that I was a vegetarian for fifteen years so I am not trying to talk you out of a veggie garden; I have one myself. You're reading this book for advice so here is what I suggest you ponder: Vegetable gardens are work to tend to and costly to set up.

In addition to that, in most parts of the country they are ugly half of the year. So, if you really just want to grow some great tasting tomatoes, why not try this approach: Go to the local farm and ranch supply and buy a galvanized tub or water trough and drill or punch some holes in the bottom. Place the tub where it gets five hours or more of sun and is out of site from the patio. Fill the container with potting soil and you have a veggie garden that will grow excellent tomatoes. Let the kids grow a few flowers so they can be farmers too. If you position this properly, you'll not have a costly garden that will be ugly half of the year or all of the year after the fun of vegetable gardening wears thin.

The other "must have" is a gazebo placed out in the far corner of the yard. The questions to ponder are as follows: First, can you build it yourself or can you afford to have it built? Second, why do you want to put the gazebo out in the corner of the yard anyway? Why not extend the patio that you have and not have to carry food and drink such a long way? Let's say that you have a fourteen foot by twelve foot patio now, but it is just not big enough. You're going to build a fourteen by twenty foot area from scratch so you have a big enough space. You already have most of the patio built and it is close to the house where you want it to be for convenience, so why not just add on to what you have? Unless you like to frantically run for the backdoor in freezing temperatures, I would suggest that the hot tub be placed under the stars, but close to the house.

Here is another example that needs to be thought out. Do we really need a big jungle gym? Here are the questions: How much time do the kids really spend outside now? Buying an expensive play set will not make them "outdoor kids," they either like being outside or they don't.

Take every idea and ask the tough questions before you start to design. Why do I want it? Can I afford it? Will it make it harder to sell the house? If you're putting the kids play area in the middle of the back yard I, and many others will be put off by this and will not buy your house. Think resale.

So, here we are in the world of reality. The good news is now we have a reasonable project that is within our budget and energy level.

Style

Much can and has been said about different landscape styles. A few common styles are the formal, Japanese, Mediterranean, Southwest, cottage garden, xeric and of course, native.   In reality, very few clients really want Japanese or formal styles once they realize that they're very high maintenance. With the exception of formal and Japanese styles, the other styles listed can be designed using this book by simply using different plants and features.

Classic southwest landscapes will usually have more cacti and succulents.

Native and xeric designs will be using plants that are native to the local area and are drought tolerant.

Mediterranean landscapes many times include Italian Cypress and topiary.

Cottages gardens are full of perennials.

Most of the country likes landscapes that are considered native, informal, Mediterranean, or cottage garden. The most practical thing to do is to use plants that do well in your area regardless of style. Forget the styles, let's go for low-maintenance and beauty.

Plant Maintenance and Turf Grass

What does low maintenance mean to me? If you are willing to spend one Saturday twice a year taking care of the yard, then that's low maintenance to me. This doesn't count mowing grass of course. If you have grass, your landscape is not low maintenance in my book. The only exception is if you have Buffalo Grass or Blue Grama Grass. Most people in the U.S. can't grow these "turf type" meadow grasses because of sandy soil, high rainfall or shade problems. These grasses are also problematic when it comes to weed resistance. Don't write to me about the wonders of these grasses. I've grown these grasses myself and they're great if drought resistance and seasonal mowing are your only concerns. If you have shade or hate weeds, then you should stay away from these grasses. If you love that thick lush feel of grass under your bare feet you won't like these type grasses.

A sure fire way to have a high maintenance landscape is to have lots of traditional turf grasses, hedges, fruit trees and if you live in a humid climate, throw in roses to really make you a lawn slave. In defense of roses, they do well in dry areas and do not have the fungal and insect problems that you see in high humidity area.

Now that I've irritated most of the horticultural community, I might as well extend my opinion on native plants as well. Unless you pick very carefully, native plants can be hard to get started. It's very easy to over water them and many times they can look brushy and unkept. Many people decide that, "they are native, so I don't need to water" and the plant dies. Once established; natives do well.

Computer Aided Design (CAD)

Here I go upsetting the computer nerds in the crowd. In my mind, computer aided design (CAD) should be computer aided drafting. CAD programs can be a fun and an interesting way to put the plan on a piece of paper, but they don't teach you to design. They may make some generic design suggestions, but very often they're frustrating and a major learning experience. My software can crash and I'll lose my work, but as long as I don't spill coffee on my paper plan I'm OK.

These landscape design software programs can be used to draw your plan, but you should still use this book for the information needed to do the design itself.

Oversized Lots

On a big lot, think big bucks and lots of time. If money and time are just not there, about the only solution is to divide the lot. Either build a courtyard and landscape only inside the smaller area, or divide the yard with screening shrubs and trees. The issue with the latter solution is that the screening will usually take some time to grow and fill in the rest of the yard. This is a tough problem as you probably bought the lot bragging about how large it is only find out that you can't afford to landscape it properly. Taking a limited budget and trying to spread it over a large area, is pretty disappointing. Try to downsize the area.

3

Designing Hardscapes and Overall Layout

Drainage
Retaining Walls
Bed Shapes
Storage Sheds
Water Features
Patios
Fire Pits
Hot Tubs
Vegetable Gardens
Play Areas
Grass Areas
Berms
Dry Creeks
Courtyards
Traffic Flow
Mulch
Working with Landscape Diagrams

Drainage

One of the hardest problems to solve in the process of landscaping is drainage. Let me give you some guidelines that will make the process easier.

First, the builder should have done this for you when the house was built, but sometimes that doesn't happen (big surprise). Or, the builder did the job right but over the years these areas filled in and changed the flow. Let's assume that we want the water to flow from the backyard around the house to the front. The toughest situation is a flat lot or a lot that has been blocked on the side yard so that water can't get around the house. You must make a decision here based on your experiences in the house and talking with the neighbors. If you and the neighbors have lived on the street for ten years and experienced heavy rainfall within that time without a problem, then you probably don't have a problem.

On the other hand, if there are a few low spots that hold water more than twenty-four hours, then I would recommend a good look at the drainage. A quick way to check the drainage as it goes down the side of the house is to look at your foundation. Foundations are always level. If you look at the foundation and see more foundation exposed at one end than the other end then the property is dropping. This is good but it may not be dropping enough.

Take the water hose and lay it in the areas in question and let the water run. (Yes, I know that we're going to waste some water, but not that much) In most areas, we don't want the water running onto the neighbor's lot, so that means that the flow needs to go around the house to the front or back. If it does so without ponding after twenty four hours, then I would say that it drains pretty well; but could still cause problems if you get a very heavy rain in a short time. Go to the door that is most likely to flood in a heavy rain and look at the step. Look to see how much the water would have to rise before it gets into the house. This distance is your "flood insurance" and this can make you feel secure or very worried. If you think that this is a problem, you need to solve it.

Let's assume that we have a spot that ponds up on the side of the house. It's natural to assume that we have a low spot, so you just fill the hole and it still won't drain. Two things can prevent drainage. First are low spots, and second are high spots. Visualize a pool table that is at a slight angle, if we poured water on the table it would drain very nicely. But if we hit the table with a sledge hammer, the hole or low spot would hold water. If we repaired the hole and then we put a small pile of soil on the pool table, we'd still have water ponding. However, it would not be from the hole it would be from the pile of soil that obstructs the flow. The moral to the story is just because the lot drops from one end to the other does not mean that the property drains without ponding. All the high and low spots will be a problem. We need a flat sloping pool table and here's how we'll get it.

First, let's visualize a U-shaped wide, shallow channel that wraps around the house. As the water enters the U, it is forced to travel around the house and out to the street. Most tract home developers use this technique and if done correctly, it will work. Sometimes the new home owner does not realize that this is why there is a low spot going around the house and either fills it in or blocks it with a patio, without installing a pipe under the patio to maintain the proper flow. Please don't do this. Whether it is done by the builder or not, what you are trying to accomplish is this U shaped drainage swale by using a poor man's transit. Don't bother to Google this because it's a phrase that I made up.

Go buy a roll of mason's string, some wood or metal stakes and a string level. A string level is just a cheap little device that attaches to a string to see if it's level. Drive stakes in the ground every fifty feet, more or less, along the route that you want the water to travel. Attach the string and add the string level. Move the string higher or lower on the stake until the string is level. Now, pull the string very tight. If the bubble moves out of level, simply inch the string up or down till it is level again. The reason that you bought mason's string is that it can be stretched tight - and this is a must. If the string sags at all, the string level will give a false reading.

Get a magic marker and make a mark on the string every foot. How high the string is from the ground doesn't make any difference as long as it is not touching the ground at any point. The string is showing you what level really looks like. This can be a shock because if you have drainage problems, the problem becomes painfully obvious.

Now, start at the high point of the yard and measure to the ground. Let's say that it measures two inches from the ground to the string. Move your tape measure to the next mark on the string and take a measurement. In a perfect world, the measurement would be two and one quarter inch and continue at that rate all the way off of your property and into the street or back alley. Before you start removing soil at a rate of one quarter inch per foot, we must see where this will take us.

Measure from the high point in the yard to the point that the drainage would flow into the street or other common ground. To make it easy, we'll say that the distance is one hundred feet. If the ground dropped at one quarter inch per foot, then the total drop would need to be twenty five inches. If you install your stakes and string all the way from the high point to the low point and level it, then you can measure the distance from the string to the ground at the high point and do the same at the low point - see if the difference is twenty five inches. If the drop is less than that, you may need to try one-eighth inch drop per foot. In my experience, a drop of less than that will not work and at this reduced drop you can't have any low spots or high spots or you will have major ponding.

The most common problem is that the front curb or street is too high. In that case, all you can do is to live with it, drain it into a low spot on your property or raise the high point in the yard. If you can tell that you have enough elevation change to make it drain, then start removing soil so that every foot that you move downhill the distance to the ground is increasing by one- eighth or one-quarter of an inch. This is most easily accomplished with a scrapping method. This is sometimes easier with a skid loader or many times a shovel will work, depending on the distance and the hardness of the ground.

In some cases, a French drain may work but it is a lot of work to install, so think about this first. What French drains do is to let the water percolate into the ground or go straight into a pipe that carries the water away. This sounds great until you realize that the water must still travel downhill to get away from the house.

Also, consider that when you put pipe in the ground you lost at least ten inches of elevation, just making it harder to get over the curb. You can add a catchment basin or even run gutters straight into the pipe, but the same physics remain; the water must go downhill. Pipe is straight and slick, so one-eighth inch drop per foot will work if the curb or street height is going to allow this.

Let's say that you ignore my advice and get the water moving in the direction that we want it to, what happens when you get to the street or curb and realize that your pipe is lower than the curb or street? Water doesn't jump and it will not go over the obstruction. The water will just sit in the pipe and back up just like a clogged sewer. All you have gained with you expense and hard work is that you don't have to worry about the water that is trapped in the pipe. One hundred feet of pipe doesn't hold enough water to make the project worthwhile, and to make matters worse, the spouse laughs at you every time it rains because the yard still floods.

One solution is to put gutters on the house. A very common mistake is to think that just putting the gutters on will solve that problem. All the gutters will do is put the water in a predictable place. It is very possible to make the problem worse because now you have concentrated all the water from the roof into a few small places. If the places where the downspouts drop the water do not drain perfectly, then all you have accomplished is moving the problem to a new location.

All areas must drain. Drainage is very important and to install a landscape without addressing this first is to flirt with flooding your house. To make it worse, many homeowner policies don't cover this.

Any property can flood! I lived in a house in Texas that was 60 feet above the river. I'll always remember the day when the river rose that 60 feet and continued to rise until it was 1 foot below my second floor! I rescued my trapped wife in my canoe. Call an engineer if you have the slightest doubt.

Retaining Walls

Now here's an interesting subject that's driven by money and practicality. Let me make a wild guess and say that most of you are doing this project yourself to save money or because you like the feeling of accomplishment. If you are trying to save money, avoid retaining walls like taxes. Even if you build the wall yourself, it will cost lots of money.

Building the wall is very labor intensive and don't diminish the back-breaking labor of backfilling behind the wall. You may need two shorter walls so it's not so imposing. The upper terraces are a no man's land. This area should be plants only unless you add steps or have a way to get a mower up on top.

You want the top of the terrace to be as low maintenance as possible. The diagrams I provided are for the lower areas of the yard, more than the tops of the terraces. Homeowners often want to put a patio up on the terrace and this is another area that requires much thought.

First, do you really want to separate your patios so that some of you guests are in a totally different part of the yard? Do you really want to carry food and drink up a set of stairs? Finally, do you have a better view up there or do you now look into the neighboring yards?

If you want the feeling of accomplishment, this is a great way to get it. But keep in mind you may be doubling or tripling the work, money and time involved. If you can easily walk up the slope, then you probably don't need a retaining wall. It is not within the scope of this book to show you how to build retaining walls. There are many great books on the subject and lots of videos on the internet.

For a natural look, stacked rock looks great and can be fun to use for the homeowner. Steps can be a challenge, but you may not need steps if you don't need access to the area very often.

Concrete is very strong, but should be faced with stone, brick or in the southwest we often use stucco. This is a wall that you will see every time you go out back or every time you pull up to the house. Pick carefully, this wall will set the mood for the entire landscape. The walls themselves can be very attractive and there are several good products to build them with.

My section of diagrams of basic plans will show you some design ideas and how best to incorporate retaining walls into your design. Good luck. I have seen some beautiful walls that were built by homeowners with the determination to pull it off. If you've made the commitment to put in retaining walls, now is the time to draw it in.

Bed Shapes

When trying to design and layout your own landscape certain shapes are commonly used by the novice. Over my thirty years of designing residential landscapes, I have been presented with many home owner designed plans. Usually they can do a pretty good job of picking plants that do well in their area if they start with a locally written plant book or use the internet to get information on what does well in their area. For reasons that are not clear, the actual bed and grass shape is what seems to cause most problems. The principles are relatively simple. Let's look at the basic shapes that we are going to use and also look at what shapes we want to avoid.

- Curved areas are soothing to the eye.
- Large flowing curves are better than tight curves.
- Perfect circles around trees and scalloped borders should be avoided.
- Straight lines, boxes, rectangles and triangles are formal and should be avoided.
- Avoid the quarter circle bed pushed into a corner.
- Raised beds can look great but add greatly to the cost and time required for the project.

In the diagram section at the back of the book, you'll see examples of the kind of shapes that work best. Experiment with these shapes to use in your project and don't be afraid to connect them to patios, retaining walls or driveways. You can enlarge them, reduce them or flip them so they extend to the left or right as needed.

Using these shapes as "islands" is a very effective way to create interest. These shapes or islands can be many different things. Islands of grass, herbs or roses work well. A good example of the use of islands and simple elegance are the greens or sand traps on a golf course. Using "islands" as negative space works well. Negative space is an area that has little or nothing in it. Rather than evenly distribute all of the plants throughout the yard, you can use this negative space to open the area up and avoid that crowded look.

The following is a list of features that will help you create your design. First lay out your "to scale" design and tape it down on the corners. Use printer paper to make a series of "cut outs' to scale. (See "scale" in Chapter 1) Make "cut outs" for a tool shed, water feature, patio, fire pit, firewood storage or anything else that you want included.

Storage Sheds

If you're going to have a storage shed, work that in first. Let's say that you don't have enough side yard to hide the storage building. What can we do? Let's take lemons and make lemonade. Decide to buy or build a storage shed that is more ascetically appealing; maybe one with windows or a little front porch that is in keeping with your style. If we must live with the shed "as is" then why not create a trellis to cover the front and then grow a vine on the trellis for that cute little cottage look?

Water Features

Unless you're building a huge, flowing waterfall, the water feature should be close to the patio so it is easier to see and enjoy. There are many videos about this subject on You Tube.

Patios

If we are going to extend the patio, some basic principles apply. First, let's figure out how many square feet we need. Look at your dining room and the furniture in it. You have your dining table and chairs, and this will be prefect for figuring some basic dimensions. Patio dining is an informal thing, unlike your dining room in the house, so let's pull the chairs back from the table and kick back like we're at an outdoor party. We need to leave room for the BBQ and at least three to four feet behind the chairs for the friends and kids to pass. As an example, a large rectangular table that seats six will need an area about fourteen by sixteen feet without the BBQ. Now, measure your existing dining area and decide the proper size for your patio.

If you need to save money and pour a smaller patio, consider going to a smaller table and/or putting the BBQ in another location, like an unused corner. Nothing is more irritating than continually scooting your chair forward to let people pass behind you. So, built your patio large enough for your needs.

Now, draw another "to scale" cut out for the patio. Consider the existing support posts on your patio when determining your square footage you need. The most efficient use of space for a patio is a rectangle or square. I know curves look great, but if the budget is tight use squares or rectangles. Curves in patios create unusable space that waste money. I like curves for grass, sidewalks and planting beds. If budget allows, the patio is where your outdoor kitchen would go. Let's keep the patio and outdoor kitchen close to the house.

Fire Pits

Fire pits can be located on uncovered patios and are great as conversation areas. Remember to design a place for the firewood that is close to the fire pit for easy access. Or, plan in a gas outlet for artificial logs.

Hot Tubs

Yes, the hot tub also needs to be close to the back door. Wet feet hitting slick concrete as you run to the house in winter can be very dangerous.

Vegetable Gardens

Place the veggies on the side of the house. Vegetable gardens look bad most of the year, so let's not make the garden too obvious. These gardens need 5 or 6 hours of full sun to do best. See chapter 2 for more details.

Play Areas

An area for the kids to play may need to be added to the plan. The side yard is the best place from an aesthetic standpoint. Mom may want to keep an eye on the kids so it may need to be in sight of the back door. A play set can be put in the grass area. However, the grass will be destroyed by the foot traffic, and mowing around the play set will be a problem. If we create a nicely shaped area filled with bark, it could be easily converted to grass, gravel or even ground cover after the kids no longer use the play set. This approach also helps you sell the house when it is time to move. A square play area in the middle of the yard will not help when it comes time to sell, so let's think curves. If you plan ahead you can make the play area work for you and protect your investment.

Now we can get started with the actual plan. Transfer your "cut outs" of the features to the final plan by tracing your cut outs. We'll put in the grass or "negative space" and paths once we have the cut outs in place

Grass Areas

In many areas of the United States, designers create bed areas for garden plants and the rest of the property becomes grass by default. For many years, I have been doing the opposite and designing the grass areas like "islands" (See Right and Wrong under the Diagrams section) with the rest of the property being used as planting beds. This approach makes it much easier to design by using enhanced and altered "kidney" and "peanut" shapes for the grass islands. This approach has the added bonus of reducing water usage and the weekly maintenance associated with large grass areas.

As our ecosystem gets dryer, the tendency is to use less grass, especially in the western U.S. Most grasses use much more water than shrubs, so trying to limit large areas of grass is very desirable. Installing sprinkler systems is much easier if you can use drip irrigation on plants and limit the installation of the much more difficult systems required by grass areas.

Berms

A berm is a little landscape hill. The most common examples of berms are those found on golf courses around putting greens. What would a putting green look like if it was flat? Now you know the value of the berm. They add dimension and interest. The trick to building a good berm is to use more soil than you think it needs. Visualize a pile of soil as it comes out of a dump truck and you will get an idea of how much you might need. Sometimes you'll get lucky, and in the process of grading you produce the soil that you need. Or, you may already have a dirt pile on your property that was getting ready to be hauled off. If you have a limited amount of soil, use it to raise the focal point in beds. If you have lots of soil, it can be used to berm all the planting areas or to contour a grass area. Be careful not to disturb your drainage.

*Tip: To keep your berm from looking like an ordinary pile of dirt,
keep raking it smooth until the edge is no longer obvious and
it tapers into the surrounding soil. If the berm looks too tall,
it probably isn't. In most cases you'll get 20 per cent
compaction and reduce the overall height.*

Dry Creeks

Landscape designers are always looking for features that can be added to the layout to make it more interesting, and if this can be done without too much expense, all the better. For years I've been designing dry creeks into my projects. If in the grading process you'll be using commercial digging equipment or if you have soil that's easy to dig, the dry creek can add a nice touch. A dry creek is a stream feature that is not designed to carry water, it's a focal point. If you add boulders or river cobble in the bottom and lots of colorful plants along the edges, then you have a very striking display.

To have much effect, the dry creek must be at least 18 inches deep and 3 feet wide along the main channel. The length of the channel needs to be at least 15 feet, not including the end basins. Your creek must have a starting point and a logical place to end. A rounded basin is a logical way to accomplish this. Form the end basins, at least 7 feet across and a little deeper than the main channel. Your creek will look more natural if it has a slow curve. If you make the creek too shallow when you put the river cobble in the bottom, it will simply fill the hole and you'll be back to level again. The excavated soil is an added bonus. Use the soil around the ends of the creek to raise the perimeter area and make the creek appear deeper. When you install decorative boulders, dig a shallow shelf for them to sit on and push the removed soil back around the boulder. This makes the boulder look like it's been there for a while rather than recently placed on top of the ground.

Don't line the creek with boulders, this is not natural nor should the boulders be all the same size. Try a grouping with large, medium and small boulders to create a natural effect. Boulders smaller than a basketball are too small to have much effect in the average yard; bigger is better. An oversized dolly works great for moving boulders. This is a great place to smash your fingers so be careful. Collect or buy boulders that look nice together and discard the mismatched junk that your neighbor wants to get rid of. Do a web search under "landscaping" then "waterfalls" and with a little searching you'll see what natural water features should look like.

Courtyards

These important areas can be very beautiful because they are generally much smaller than the rest of the yard. Due to their limited size, grass, paths, and edger are not a concern and the focus is on plants. Sometimes I am asked to design a small patio for these areas and occasionally a water feature. If the budget is not too tight, then this is an area that will benefit from these hardscape features.

But let's think this through. Do you really need a patio out in front of the house? Our culture has changed over the years and the front porch is no longer the social meeting place that it once was. Many clients never see their front door because they drive into the garage and enter the house through an interior door. Some of my clients also pick up the mail from a centralize mail box as they enter the subdivision, so the front yard is only seen by the occasional visitor. That being said, the front of the house should be attractive but if money and time is a factor, then this is a place to consider limiting cost.

In some parts of the U.S., courtyards are very popular and can be quite large. I have landscaped many that were over 2,000 square feet. Once you get to that size, the principles for landscaping entire yards apply to these courtyards. If you have a courtyard in the back of the house, this is a place to pull out the stops. A little money and time spent here can result in a wonderful landscape that is easy to maintain because of the reduced size.

Traffic Flow

Now that you have decided the location of your features and beds, let's use flowing curved paths to connect the features so they fit into your customized plan. We need paths to the side gates, tool shed, vegetable garden, and to add interest and "break up" large areas of the yard. Most clients want to create paths with concrete. Let's go back to the budget and consider cost vs. need. How often do you travel that path? How mobile are you? Will you live out your life in this house? If you are using the path daily, have enough money and are going to retire in the house, by all means put in concrete sidewalks. For safety, you should make them at least four feet wide. If you think that you might wind up in a wheelchair at some point, add in concrete ramps while you're pouring the concrete. If you seldom travel that path, are in good health and will be moving to another house in the next few years, is this worth the money and effort?

If you still want the path but need to save money, how about a mulch or crusher fines (also called decomposed granite) path. Let's avoid the "old fashion" concrete stepping stones if we can. Very large flagstone slabs work great and look expensive. Little pieces of flagstone are hard to walk on and look utilitarian. You can't make cutouts for the paths, so use a piece of tracing paper to experiment with the sidewalks.

The two basic rules on sidewalk or path shape are don't make them straight, and don't make them too scalloped. Gentle curves that follow the beds look best. Now we have the basic hardscape designed; the bed areas a laid out and the connecting paths are in. We're ready for plants.

Mulch

After the plants are in, we need to decide on the mulch for our project. So, what the heck is mulch? Compost, crusher fines, decomposed granite, bark, pecan shells, colored shredded tire rubber and colored gravels are all examples of the mulch material that are commonly used in the U.S. (I've also seen tumbled colored glass used, but let's not get weird.)

This is very important in that it will alter the look of everything that you have worked so hard to pull together. You can use different mulches in different beds but be very careful here. You're usually going to be better off with no more than two choices.

Keep in mind if you have grass, the color and/or texture of the grass is strong. If you have paths, this adds another color and texture. When I use grass and colored paths in designs, I usually just add one color/texture of mulch. If you add more than two types of mulch, the area will start to look busy.

TIP: In areas of high wind, bark can blow away!

In the southwest, gravel is used as a poor substitute. Stringy shredded bark is great because the long stringy pieces interlock and keep it in place. If you pick it up and it can run it through your open fingers, then it will also blow around in very high winds.

No mulch is perfect for all situations. Use 2 to 4 inches of these products for best results.

Working With the Landscape Diagrams

At this point you should already have your retaining wall, if needed, along with the patio, shed or other features in place. Take a look at the "typical plans" and pick out a design or two that appeal to you. Ignore the plants on the plan. We're just looking at the general layout of the beds and grass area to see if it roughly fits your lot or can be altered to fit your lot. Keep in mind that the grass area may not be grass at all, it can be "negative space" (without plants) that can be mulch, gravel, or the kids play area. As you alter the plan, be sure to look at the page that shows you the basic dos and don'ts when it comes to shapes. This should help with the alterations. Put tracing paper over your design paper and roughly sketch in the design you like. Remember, none will be perfect! Make some of the curves bigger or smaller to fit into the design that you are creating and to accommodate the cut out features you have included. Now is when your creativity kicks in and you begin to make the changes to accommodate your property. Single trees can be in grass areas, but avoid having too many trees to mow around. Groups of trees work best if you can put them in beds. To do this, you may need to enlarge or reduce the size of an area to make room. Try to keep your bed at least three foot wide at the narrowest point. Work with these shapes and rotate them, or even flip them until you find a shape that can fit without much alteration.

There are two parts of the process that are the most difficult for most people, and you have just completed the first one. Take one more look at the plan to be sure that this layout is ready for your plants. If you change your mind beyond this point, you'll have to start all over. This is also a great time to ask for input from friends or family. Be aware that family or friends may want to redesign the whole thing to "help." Only listen to the practical reasons why the design needs to be altered. All you really want from them is specific reasons why the design is not right. If they remind you that you need to leave room for the BBQ, then that's something you should listen to, but if they just don't like the plan and don't have any real reason why, then you might want to just go with your gut. We've worked too hard at this point to listen to baseless negativity. At this point, you know more about landscape design than they do.

4

Designing with Plants

Plant Selection

Now we're really having fun. Plant selection is the most fun and easiest part of our project for most people and here is where the secret of my process really takes shape. This is a new way for most laymen and professionals to think and it works very well if you follow the process.

Think as though you were an artist and you are getting ready to paint. You'd get out the paints that you think you might need for the project without thinking about where they'd be used on the canvas. You may use all the colors or you may not. Just like the painter doesn't think about where they might use a color, we won't think about where the plants might go as we pick them. We're just collecting a plant palate that we like.

Pull out your book or website with its plant list. (See "What Do I Need" in Chapter 1). Your book or website has done some of the work for you. The list is probably already divided into trees, shrubs, perennials, groundcovers, annuals and so forth. If it is also divided into a sun plants list and a shade plants list, then that's even better. Pick your plants from these lists, but keep in mind some of the following thoughts as you pick.

We probably want a year round landscape, so let's pick some shrubs that keep their leaves in the winter. If you pick all colorful perennials, your landscape will be wonderful in the warm parts of the year and dead looking the rest of the time. If you take that approach you'll also have to cut back the entire landscape in the winter. Many plants look great when they're in bloom, but do you really like the plant when it's not in bloom?

Most people have a tendency to think in terms of colors. We'll design based on height and width, and then color will be considered last. It does no good to have the colors you want in groups if the group looks unorganized because of poor placement. Organize by height, and then work on color. Most women think that designing the landscape is like interior design, and sometimes that's true. One of the main differences is color. Man-made colors can clash very easily, but natural colors seldom do. I'm an avid outdoorsman and I've spent countless hours wandering in nature. I never remember looking at a natural landscape and saying "That bush sure does clash with that tree." Natural colors are very forgiving and it's hard to makes mistakes here. I realize that many books have been written on the subject of coordinating color in the landscape. Monet is probably turning over in his grave, but he was a painter and we're landscape designers, so let's not worry about it.

What greatly complicates the color issue is the fact that the plants won't necessarily be blooming at the same time, so does color coordination really matter as much as you thought? My point is this is a place that can make a new designer crazy, but it's not as important as you might think. That being said, if you're willing to spend the extra time to work with the colors, you can produce great results.

This is a good time to make note on the plan as to north. North facing walls will be in relative shade all day and very cold. South and west walls will be sunny and hot. East facing walls will get morning sun and afternoon shade. Many plants do well on north walls especially plants that don't like afternoon full sun.

If you have an average size lot then you probably don't need more that 5 plants from any one group. Pick about 3 trees, 5 shrubs, 5 perennials, 2 vines and a couple of species of groundcovers.

Picking Large Trees

Let's look at trees first. Trees are the most important part of the landscape and several things need to be considered here. First is overall size, large trees produce lots of shade and that can be great or cause problems. If they're large shade trees, the problem is that they start out so small that the surrounding plants are in full sun and in a few years the same plants may be in full shade. If you can't work around this problem then you are stuck with plants that do well in both situations. Several answers come to mind. You could plant a smaller tree that does not create very much shade. You can also minimize the shade if you plant your shade tree on the north end of the property. Now it shades your neighbor. You should discuss this with the neighbor before planting. Remember in most places, the neighbor owns the "air space" above their property and that means that they could cut all the limbs straight up from the property line and ruin your tree. Or worst yet, their brother-in-law is a lawyer and you know how that goes.

One of the best answers is to use smaller ornamental trees and place them so you get the shade where you want it, without shading the whole landscape. Keep in mind that at some point you will be picking perennials and wanting color and most colorful plants like sun. You've been warned.

Picking Ornamental Trees

Smaller trees can be placed closer to the house; they can help to screen unwanted views and are more likely to bloom. Many times they'll have foliage closer to the ground than shade trees and make it easier to screen that big motor home that your neighbor just bought. Think of a shade tree as the roof or your landscape and ornamental trees are the walls.

Now, what's my definition of an ornamental tree? Any shrub over 10' can be considered an ornamental tree for the sake of design. Take a Lilac for example: Most people probably think of a Lilac as a large shrub, but if it's 12' tall it's a tree as far as your design is concerned. If you trimmed the lower limbs and foliage like many people do to large Crape Myrtles, then you'll begin to see that it looks like a tree even if it's 10 feet tall. A tree has a very vague definition as compared to a large shrub.

When picking trees, consider the leaf size. If your top pick tree has ten thousand leaves and they're the size of a dime, as compared your second choice that has leaves the size of a dinner plate, then which one will the "leaf raker" in your life want. (Or, the downwind neighbors for that matter.)

If you want fruit trees, you might as well purchase a sprayer and insecticide at the same time. Fruit trees sound great but the same people that love the fruit tend to hate chemicals so ponder that for a while.

Fruit trees in general are messy and short lived. I planted an apple, a plum and a cherry in a moment of weakness at my house in New Mexico. I want my fig tree back that I had in Texas. It was easy to grow, disease resistant and produced copious amounts of fresh figs...yum! Some fruit trees are better than others.

Finally, shallow roots can be a real problem but a good plant source or the local nursery can warn you away. Keep in mind that some shallow rooted trees can be very fast growing and are desirable for people with large properties, where they can be planted far enough away from the sidewalks and foundations. Sometimes shallow rooted trees can be used as a backdrop to the rest of your plantings without causing problems.

Your trees will produce shade under the tree and to the north side of the canopy due to the angle of the sun in the northern hemisphere. You may want to make a simple note on the plan as to where the shade vs. sun areas are to use as we lay out the plants.

Also, keep in mind that some of the plants that like sun will eventually be in part shade. Most sun plants will do OK as they get less sun over time because they slowly adjust to the part shade. Since the plants are approaching maturity, at this point maximum growth from perfect sun conditions is not as important. Some plants must have full sun all the time and a note on those plants would be helpful as you design. If the information on the plant says "sun to part shade," you can usually work with those plants easier because their light needs are more versatile. Are we having fun yet?

Read the overall spread of the trees that you want to use. Let's say that the tree you like is 20 feet across at maturity. If this is more shade than you wanted, then pick a smaller tree. It's very easy to see that the trees can quickly give you more shade than you may want on your plants. Most plants that bloom heavily will want at least full morning sun. Now, let's be realistic and say that it is very difficult to do a great design if you get too carried away with the sun vs. shade thing. Most shade plants can take some sun especially in the morning and most sun plants don't need sun all day. An average city lot may only need one or two shade trees or one or two ornamental trees. Larger lots, or if you want lots of shade, you will need more trees. Pick your trees.

Picking Shrubs

These plants should be selected and sorted into groups based on size and sun requirements. Most shrubs don't produce enough shade to cause major problems, so in most cases we only need to be concerned with the sun they need, not the shade they produce.

Select the shrubs that you want to use and group them into two groups; tall shrubs and shorter shrubs. Then make a little note as to sun, shade, or partial sun/partial shade. If you're putting in a lot of shade trees, then picking shrubs that can take shade is very important. Make a note as to which shrubs are evergreen or deciduous (loses leaves in winter). If you don't go outside in the winter, this may not be very important, but in warmer climates where you can sit outside in the winter, it's more important. If you like to open the window coverings in the winter, it's nice to see foliage rather than a cold and leafless look. Now, we have the shrub list done.

Picking Vines

Our next subject is vines and the main thing here is to understand that many vines want to take over the other plants, and it can be high maintenance to keep them under control. I suggest using vines that stay within bounds to accent portions of a fence or wall where height is needed, but width is not.

Climbing roses are a great choice in areas of low humidity because many of them will spread less than twelve feet. Carefully check the spread before deciding on a variety or rose.

Also, note that some vines are "footed" meaning they have roots that'll attach themselves and harm brick, stone, or stucco walls. Some vines will require a trellis and others will naturally stay on a fence without added support.

It's very important to know if the vine is deciduous (loses its leaves in winter), evergreen or dies to the ground every year. Vines that die back, even if it's not all the way to the ground, will add maintenance due to the annual trimming needed. Most vines can also be used as ground cover and several species of vine can be used in shady areas under groups of trees where it is hard to grow other plants. Now, pick your vines.

Picking Ground Cover

This is another class of plants that form a vague group. For our purposes, any vine or shrub less than two feet tall can also be put in the groundcover group. (Plants can be in more than one group depending on who you're asking). Divide your ground covers into sun or shade plants; just like the others and pick on that basis.

Picking Perennials

Finally, we get to the most fun plants of all. Perennials are plants that suffer "die back" after freezing conditions. Perennials generally bloom the longest and grow the fastest, making them great plants to watch as they return every spring. That full and colorful cottage garden look that you see in gardening magazines is usually the result of perennials. Why not just plant all perennials? If all you had were perennials, then the landscape would be very bare in the winter. Adding perennials is the economical way to have color without having to replant annuals twice a year. Divide your perennial by height and shade tolerance.

This is a good place to take an overall look at the colors we've picked. Remember that the bloom colors you see in books or on websites may be just one of many colors that are available. Now you have your plant palate. Hang on to this list - it's the backbone of your design. At this point, your plant list should be complete.

Plant Groups

When I do designs and tell the client how many plants I've used, they sometimes think that I've used too many plants. What they don't realize is that the plants are designed to grow into groups so that the foliage and blooms are intensified. A single flower is pretty, but a bouquet of the same flower is much more appealing. A few single plants spaced around the yard will have no intensity or apparent design. You must have groups to add intensity. Using this approach, a yard with fifty plants will appear as fifteen or less groups as the planting matures.

When you begin to draw your plant groups, the circles should touch if they are of the same species. It would seem that the plants would over-grow each other and cause a problem. The fact is that plants of the same species are spaced this way by designers on a regular basis so that the plants grow into the groups we are after. On the other hand, more space will be needed between groups of the same species because we don't want plants of different species to overgrow each other. You'll notice that when it's first installed, your design won't look as organized as it does when the groups grow together.

The client that wants that "floral bouquet" look that is commonly seen in many gardening magazines must use lots perennials. This can be very attractive, but use this technique sparingly in focal points because it increases the number of plants that must be cut back in the off season. Because of the severe pruning and resultant foliage loss, these areas will look very sparse in the winter.

Roofs and Walls

The first plants to add are the trees. You can make many mistakes in the plant part of the design and recover easily, but the trees are the most important. Follow the guidelines that I gave you for the trees. Pay special attention to the shade information. Keep referring back to the templates and pay special attention to all the little tips. Always remember that too much shade requires you to also love the plants that can grow in the shade you are creating. Single trees can go in the grass areas, but avoid putting lots of trees in the grass because they are hard to mow around. If you're not careful, you can also produce too much shade for the grass.

Draw in the trees using a compass to make a circle the size of three quarters of the mature plant. A tree that gets twenty feet across at maturity will need a circle that represents about fifteen feet. At one quarter scale, that is a circle three and three quarters of an inch. Just hold the compass alongside the scale and adjust it till it is at the fifteen foot mark.

Why are we not drawing the plants at their mature size? First, some plants may never reach that size due to soil, sun, and watering variations. Secondly, if you give every plant room to grow to its maximum mature size, then your landscape will look very sparse for many years. You must also consider the source of the information. In the south, a Photinia will grow to eighteen feet, but in the desert a Photinia is likely not going to get much larger than ten feet.

The plant's size can vary a lot within each species, so you just have to make some estimates and three quarters mature size is about as good as you can expect. One trick is once the plants get to the size you want, start seeing how little water you can use and still keep the plant looking healthy. This will stunt many plants and help control unwanted growth.

Focal Points

Focal points can be in corners, wide bed areas or isolated areas that we'll soon discuss. Before you start putting in plants, you need to have an idea where you want your focal point to be. Every design needs a focal point that is extra special. The focal point should have special features, maybe you want that over-planted "cottage garden" look with lots of color, or even a combination of the two. Using the "frontal elevation" to help visualize the focal points is very helpful.

Narrow Places

Some places that are narrow or isolated can use unique plants. Vines work great along narrow bed areas where you need height but not width. If you don't need height but the bed is narrow, you can use short shrubs, groundcovers or perennials. Avoid thinking that you can just trim the plant to fit the space; this will increase your maintenance and not look natural. Avoid hedges, they're old school and formal!

Tip: The more you trim, the more unnatural a plant looks and the higher the maintenance. Pick a plant that gets the size you need and cut back (pun intended) on the work, not the plant.

Isolated Areas

Bed areas that are isolated but still highly visible can be very interesting. Rather than thinking like a florist, think like an art gallery owner that wants to really make a statement in the entrance of the gallery. We need a specimen plant or feature. Now is where you use that plant or feature that has special meaning. Yuccas, palms, ornamental grasses, beautiful pots, water features, a boulder or even a sun dial will work. These may also be used in your focal point. Many times these specimens look great surrounded by your smallest, but most colorful plant selections.

Tip: If you need electricity for your feature,
this is where you stop and call the electrician.

Plant Placement

Let's face it, I can't design this for you plant-by-plant, but you can design it if you follow these directions. Just use the following guidelines and diagrams and you'll see that you can do a really good job.

So, here we are ready for the plants. Our plan is drawn "to scale," the features that we wanted to add are in place, and we think we're happy with the bed layout. We've decided whether or not we want to install grass and we've positioned it on the plan.

Draw your plants at three quarters of their mature width. If your plant information source list the plant as getting four foot wide at maturity (and you're drawing in one quarter inch scale) then use a three quarter inch circle to represent that plant. (at three quarters its mature width) Most shrubs and perennials will get between two foot and six foot wide so most of your plant circles will be one half inch for the small ones to one and a half inch in diameter for the large ones. Make your plant circles touch if they are the same species just like the sample plans. Leave a little more space between plants of different species.

The Plant Design

Let's start with a couple of definitions before we put in the plants.

"Bird's eye view" means the view from above.

"Frontal elevation view" is the way you would view the planting from a standing position.

Think in the "frontal elevation view' and then draw it in the "bird's eye view." (see plans in back) .

Even though we're visualizing as a frontal elevation, we're drawing as a bird's eye view so that we can get our plant spacing right and be able to measure grass, mulch, or gravels.

When it comes to the plants, the following is the most important part of the design process. Read it until you thoroughly understand it.

Get out the landscape plans at the back of the book and make a copy of several of them for easy reference. At this point, the bed layouts are not important and you're only looking at the plants. If you look carefully you'll see that there are patterns to the groupings. You'll be drawing similar groupings but doing it one plant at a time, using the plants from your personalized list. Here is how it works:

Get out the sample plans and your plant list to refer to as you design.

First, I put in my shade trees, being careful not to put in so many trees that I "shade out" the other sun loving plants on my list. If most of the plants on your list are sun loving, this is a good place to think less shade or more shade loving plants! Next, I put in my ornamental trees.

Now, let's look at the narrow areas of the beds along the walls and fences. These are areas for your vines to cover the fences or very small plants to cover the ground. It's very difficult to find a good selection of plants like Nandinas that'll grow tall without getting the unwanted width for these narrow areas. I know that you could put in a plant and trim it, but then you'd increase your maintenance and worse yet, you'd have designed a formal, boxy looking landscape.

Next, let's consider a mass planting of ground covers or vines under the trees. Often plants like English Ivy or Columbine can take the shade that your trees will produce, and fill these sometimes difficult areas.

Finally, let's put in the shrubs and perennials. I put in one species at a time. For example, if I'm putting in Abelias that get five feet tall, I'll put in all the Abelias at the same time. My thinking is this; the Abelia is a fairly large shrub, so I put it at the back of the beds first. If I have a Dwarf Indian Hawthorn on my list, I put the Hawthorns in front of the tall Abelias. It is important to constantly refer back to the sample plans.

Next, I would put in the smaller shrubs, and finally the perennials for color. I'm simply grouping the tall shrubs at the back and adding smaller shrubs and perennials at the front of the bed. As I do this, I'm making sure that I watch the shade issue. As you design, stop and use the frontal elevation view to visualize what you are doing. Now, look at your bloom colors, if the plants are blooming at the same time and they clash, all you need to do is substitute for the bloom color you want. Change to any other plant of the same approximate size.

Since you have used my technique to separate your plants by size and sun requirements, at this point you should have very few changes to make, if any. Label your plants and you're done!

5

Plans and Instructions

We'll use the following key to make design suggestions for each of the landscape plans that follow. You probably won't be able to just pick out a plan and use it "as is". We want to design a custom plan for your property and your specific needs.

First, pick the plan that's closest to your lot, house and hardscape lay out. Don't be afraid to flip it over if that view is closer to your situation.

Next, alter it using the instructions and suggestions under "Designing Hardscapes" in Chapter 3 to create your personalized hardscape design.

Finally, you'll be designing the plant layout using a combination of the instruction under "Designing with Plants" found in Chapter 4 and the following plans. The lettered circles on the plans will apply to all of the plans. To keep the plan from getting too cluttered, only one plant in a group is labeled, but use the same plants to complete the group. You'll be able to design the plant portion by paying close attention to these plans and especially the lettered circles. The lettered circles are suggestions only and included to help you decide what possible plants to use. Constantly refer back to your list of plants that can be used based on height and shade tolerance. This'll make better sense when you get started.

A   Consider small to medium shrubs in this area.

B   Consider medium to large shrubs in this area.

C   Consider a large shrub or small tree in this area

D   Consider a vine or groundcover in this area.

E   Cover the ground with 3"-4" of mulch

F   Consider a bench, a grouping of pottery, a statue, a birdbath, a small water feature, a fire pit or even a boulder in this area.

G   This area can be grass, ground cover, mulches, a play area or gravel with weed barrier.

H   This is the patio possibly with an outdoor kitchen, hot tub, and/or fire pit.

I   This is a border in case you have grass adjacent to this area.

J   Consider perennials or small shrubs in this area.

K   Consider an ornamental tree or a shade tree.

L   Consider putting the storage shed, dog run or vegetable garden in this area.

M   Consider a path in this area.

N   Consider medium shrubs in this area.

O   Consider a bridge in this area.

P   Consider large flagstone slabs in this area.

Q   Existing trees

R   Consider a vine in this area on the ground.

S   Consider a berm in this area.

T   Consider if you need a retaining wall here.

U   Consider a play area here.

V   Consider a dry creek in this location.

W   Consider boulders in this area.

6
Landscape Diagrams

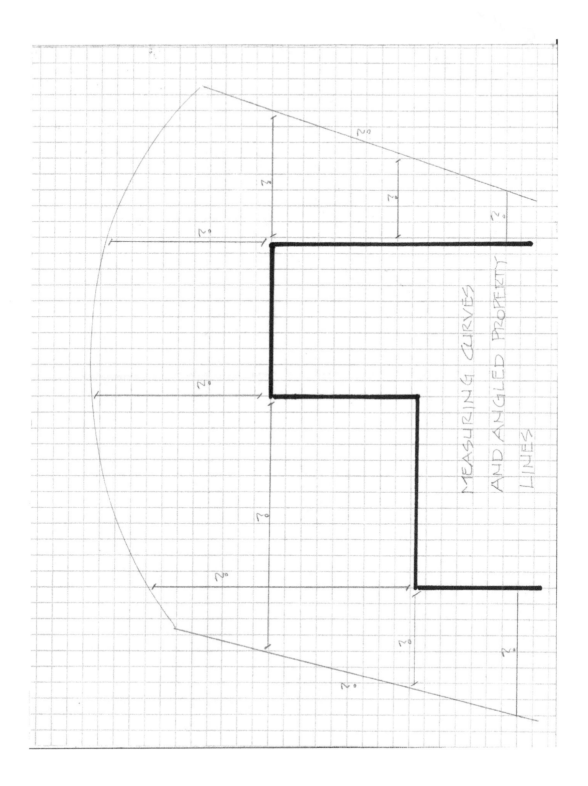

N

FRONTAL ELEVATION

BIRD'S EYE VIEW

SAME DESIGN

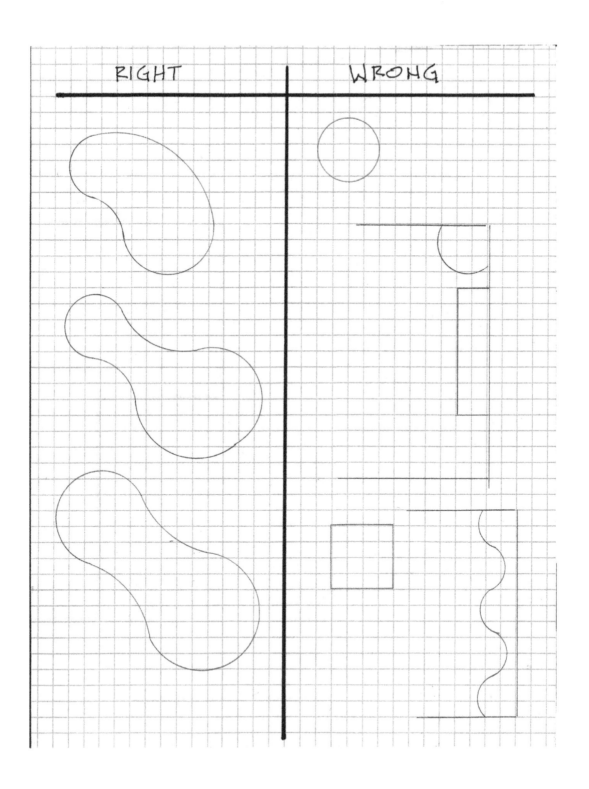

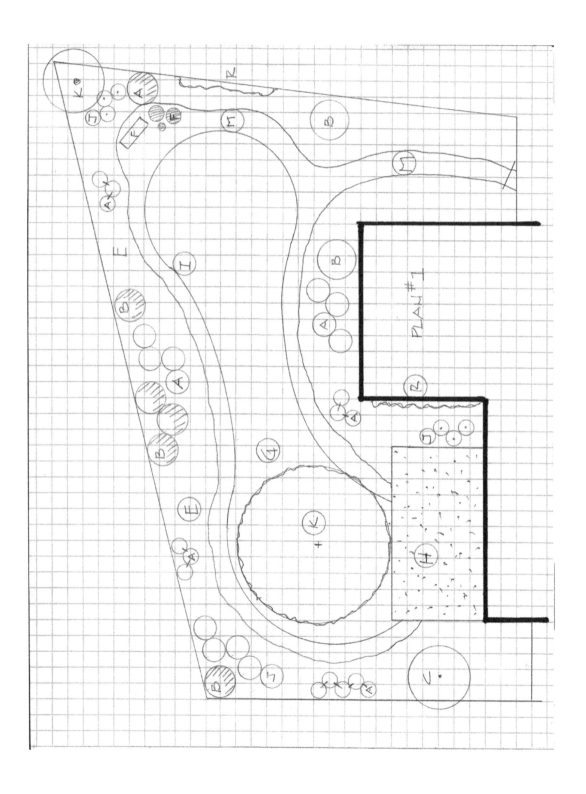

PLAN #1

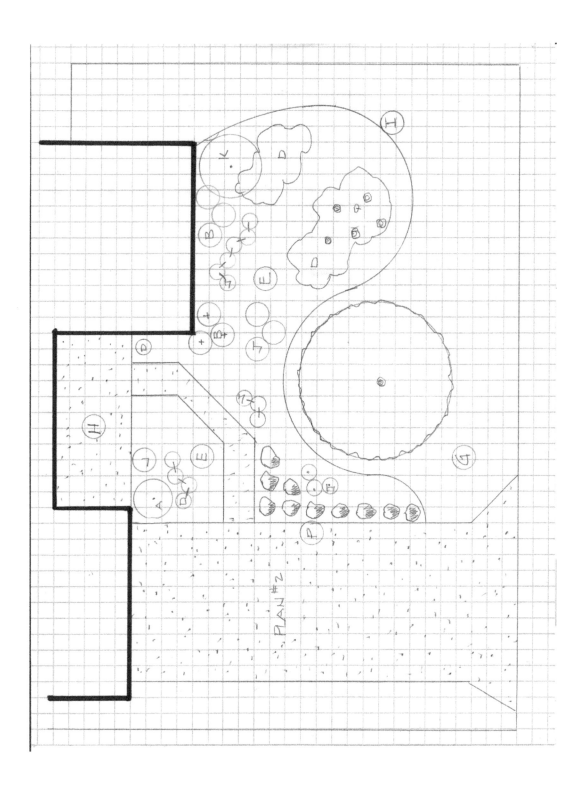

PLAN #2

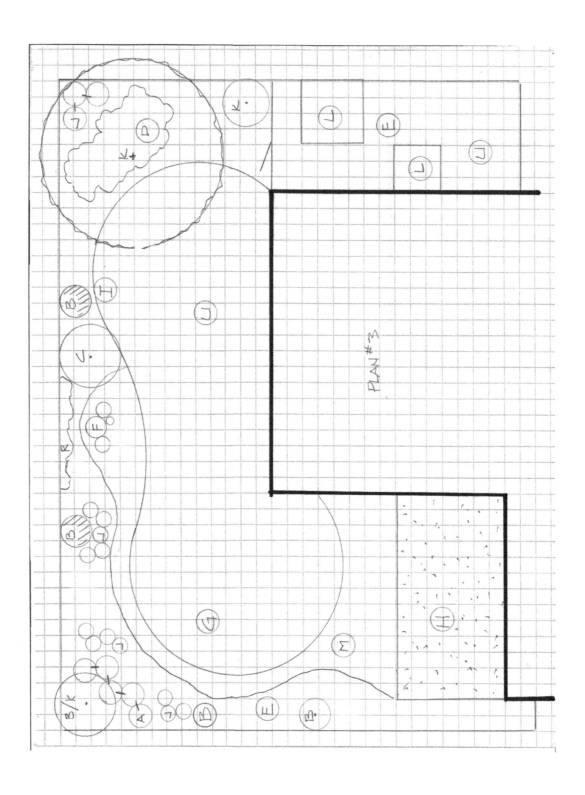

PLAN #3

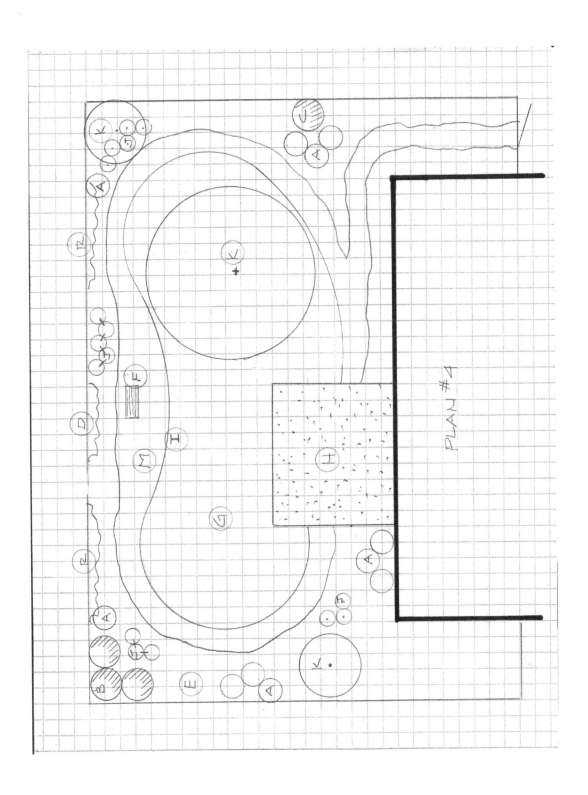

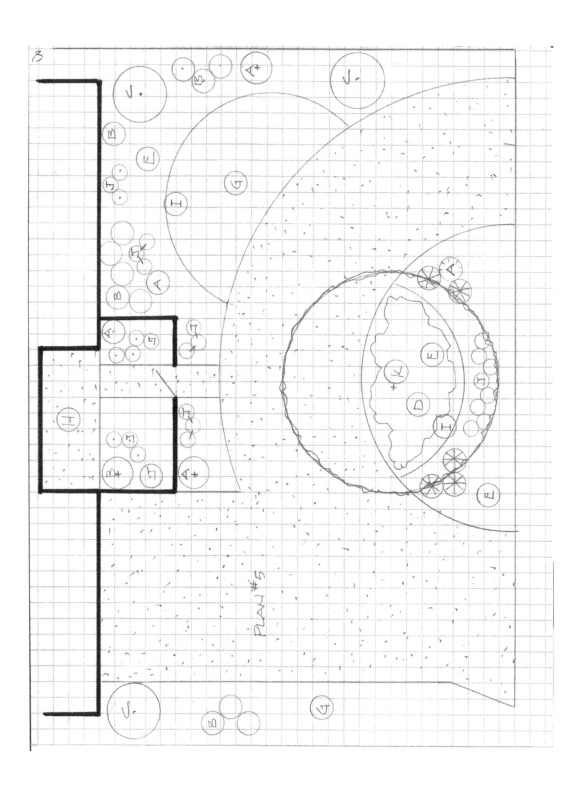

PLAN #5

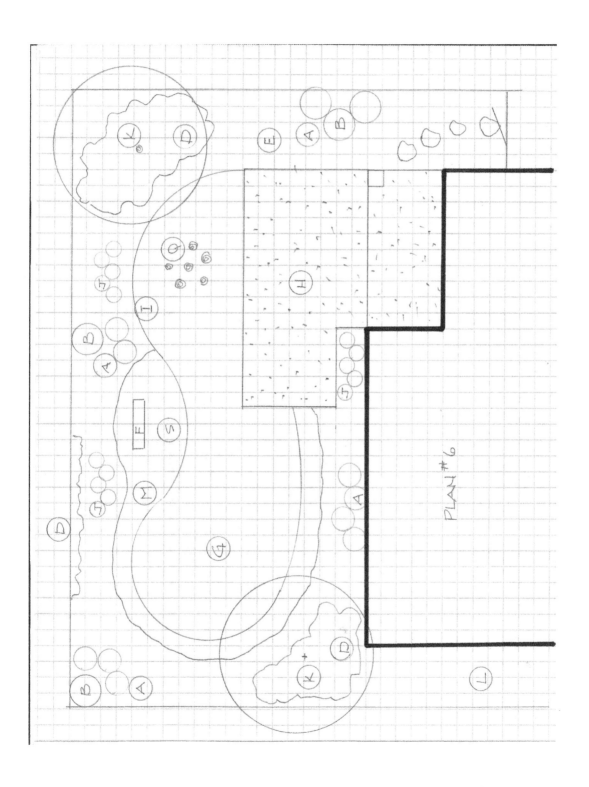

PLAN #6

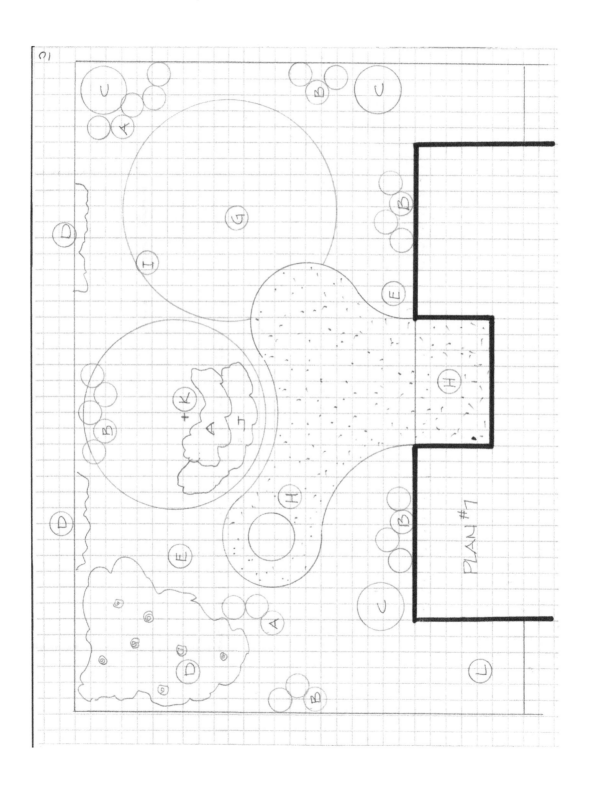

PLAN #7

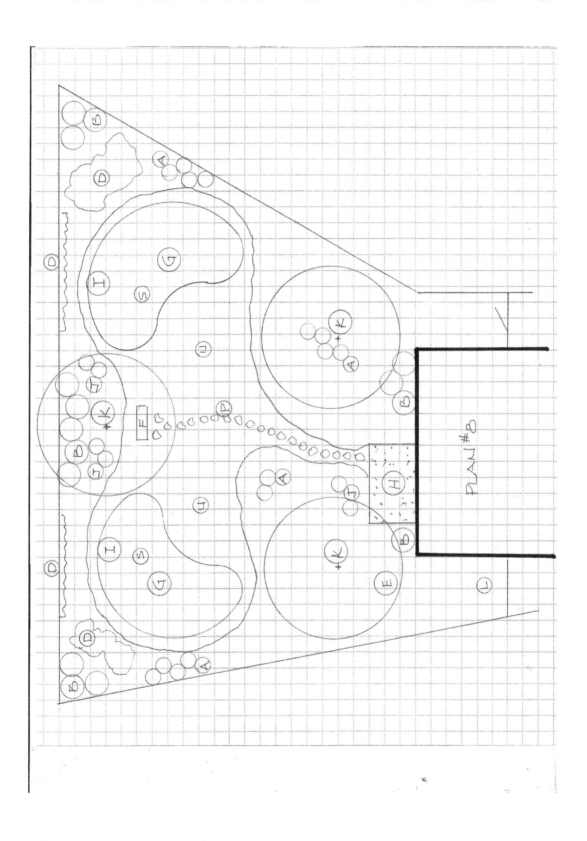

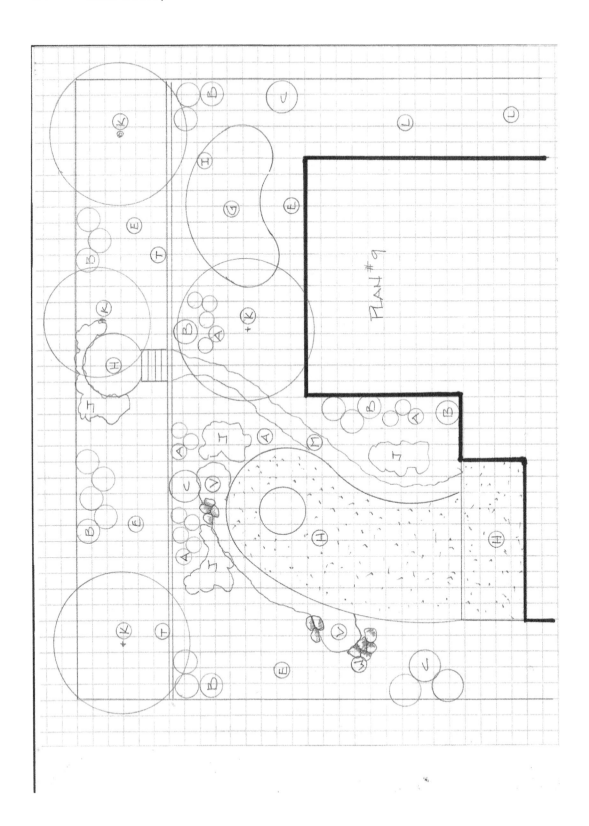

PLAN #9

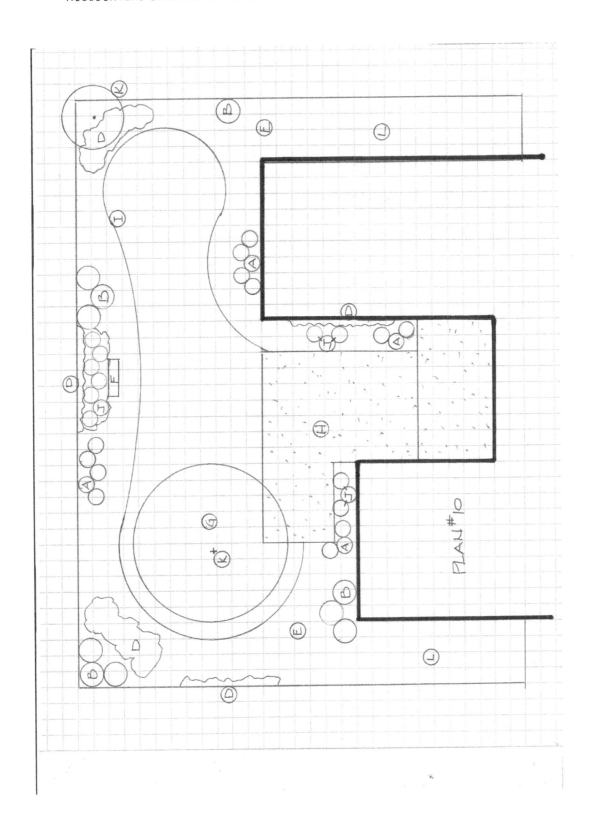

PLAN #10

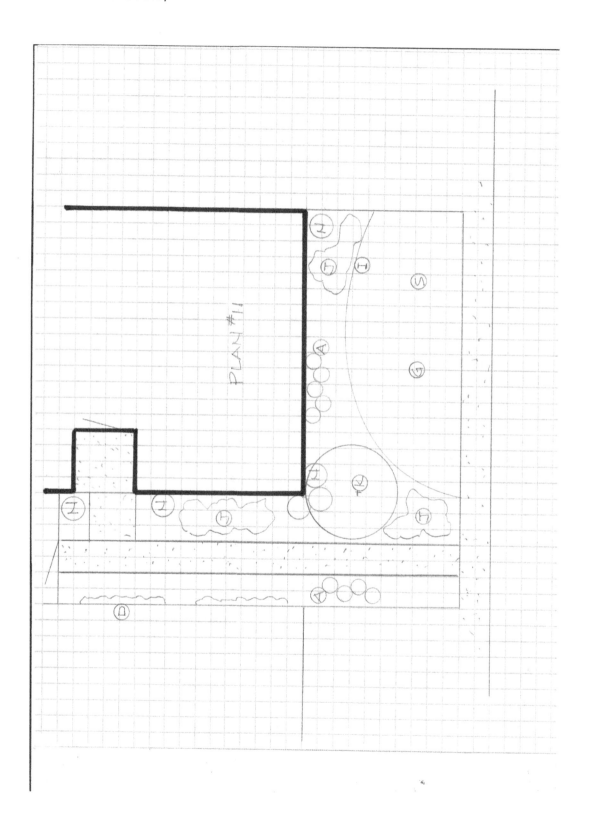

PLAN #11

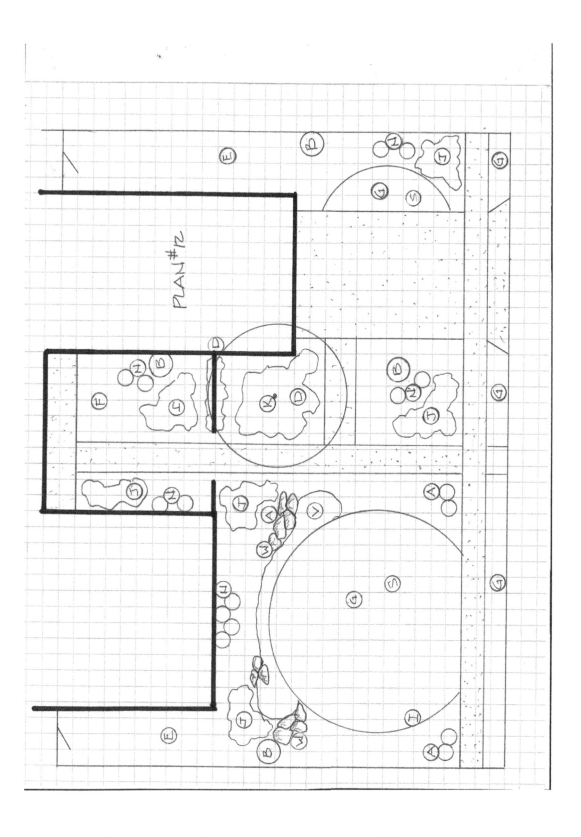

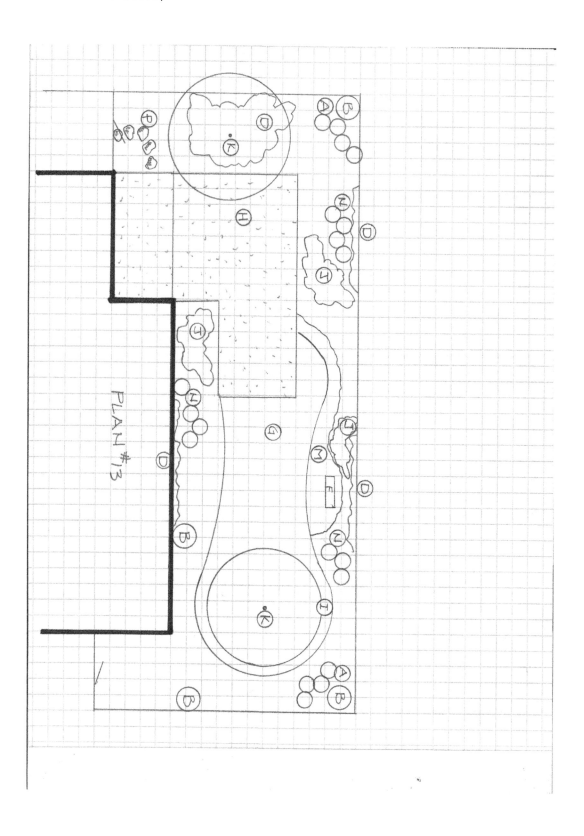

PLAN #13

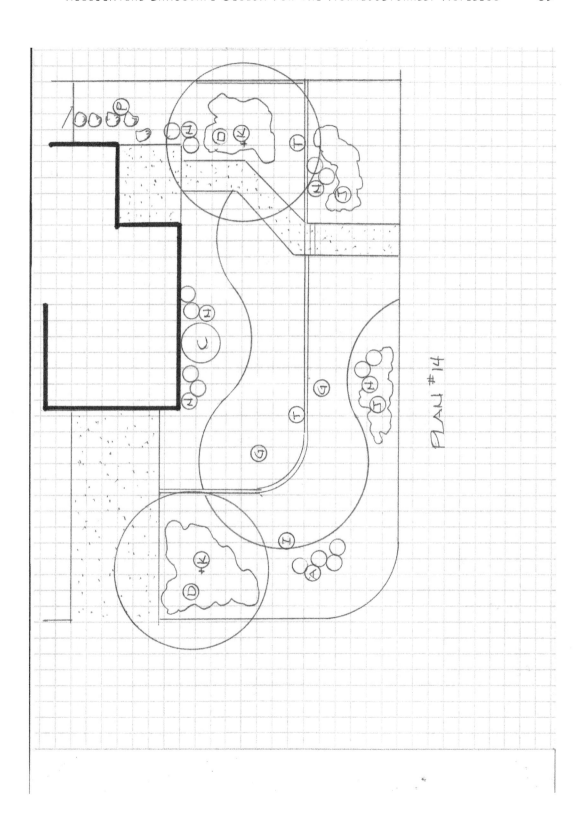

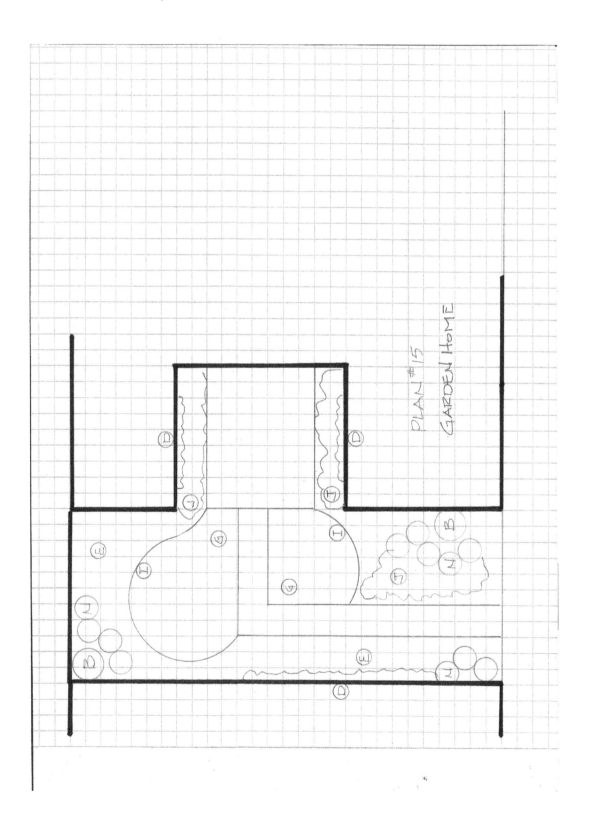

PLAN #15

GARDEN HOME

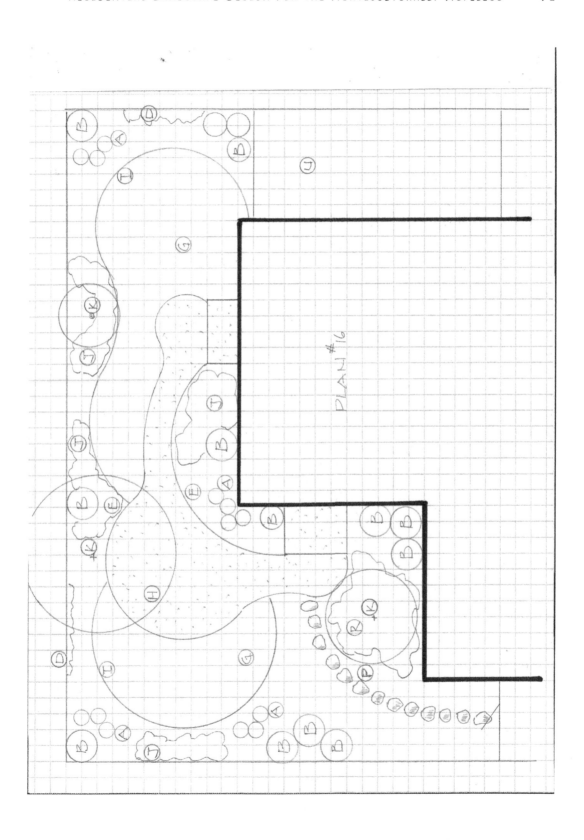

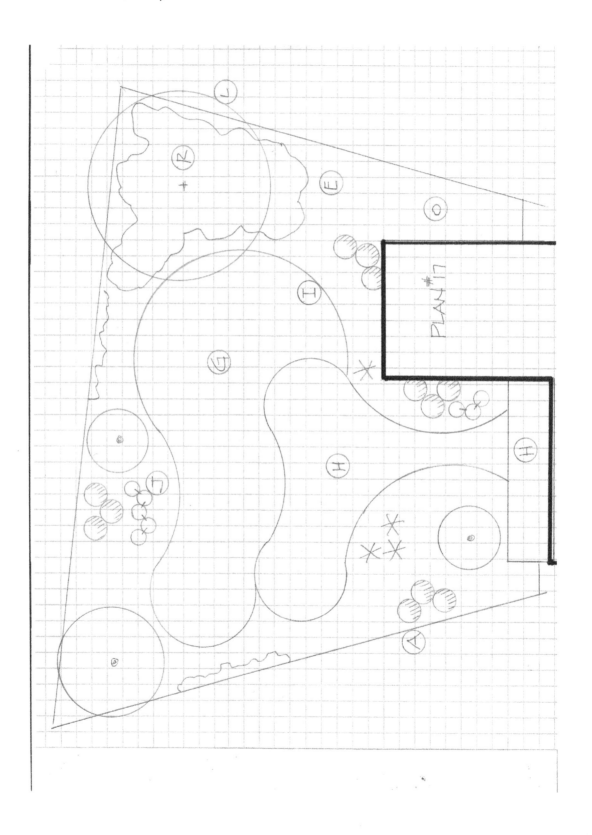

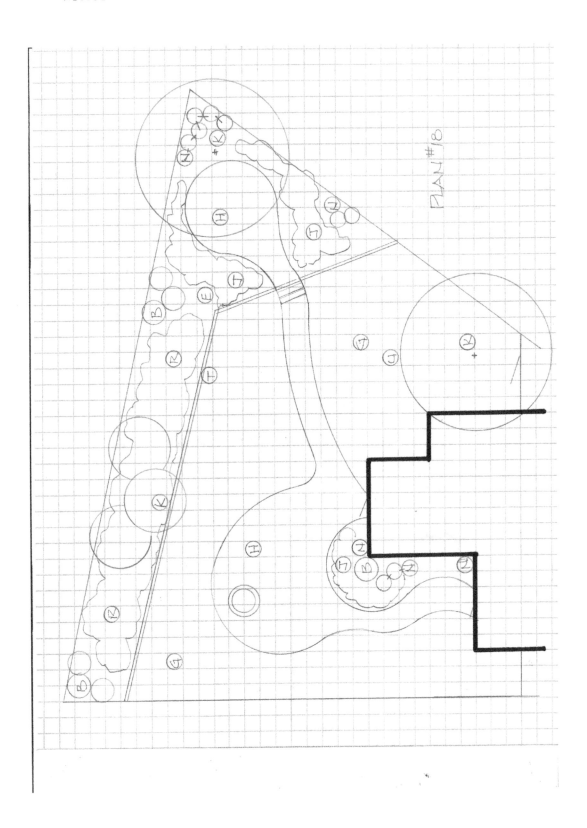

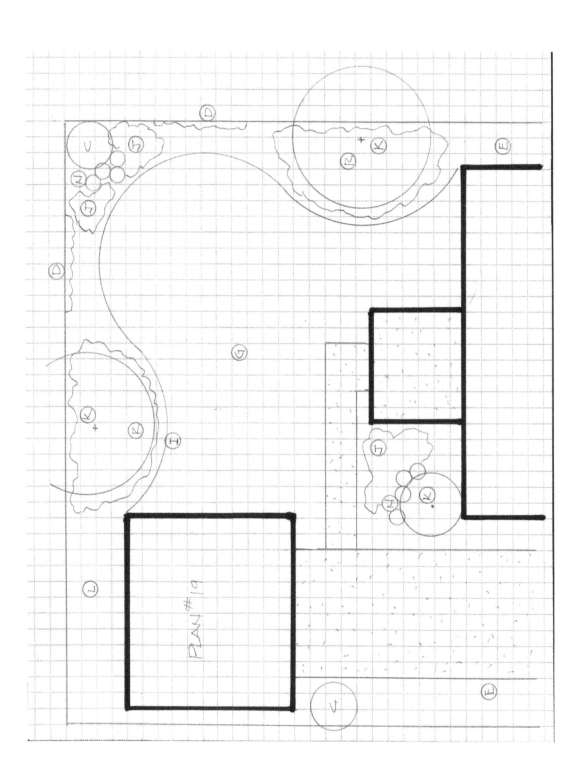

PLAN #19

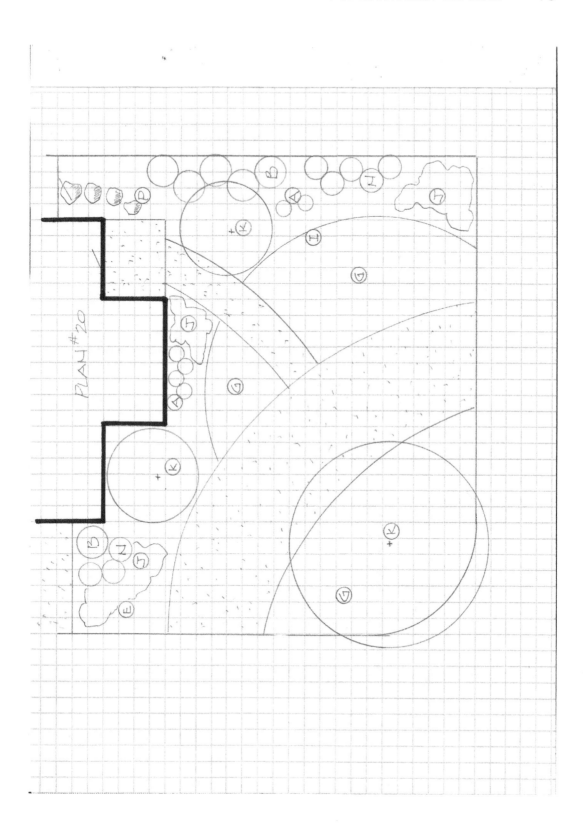

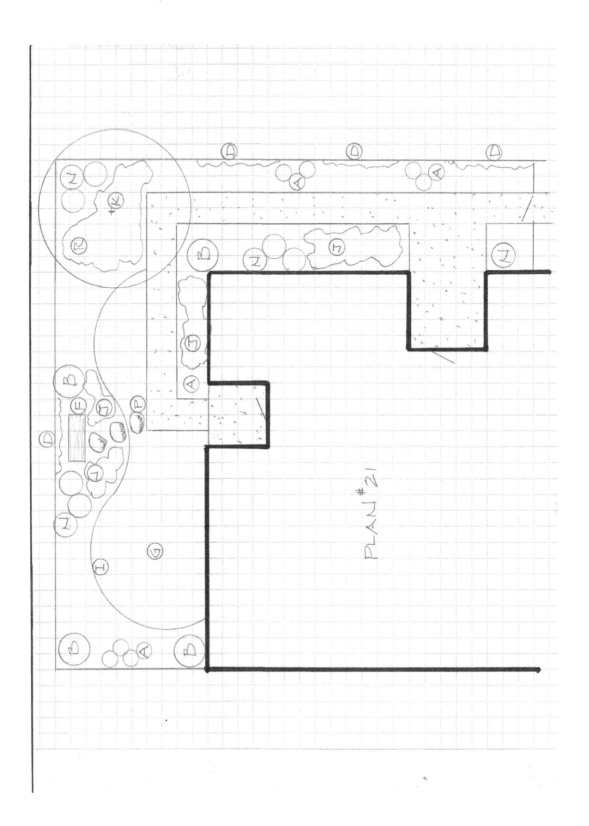

PLAN #21

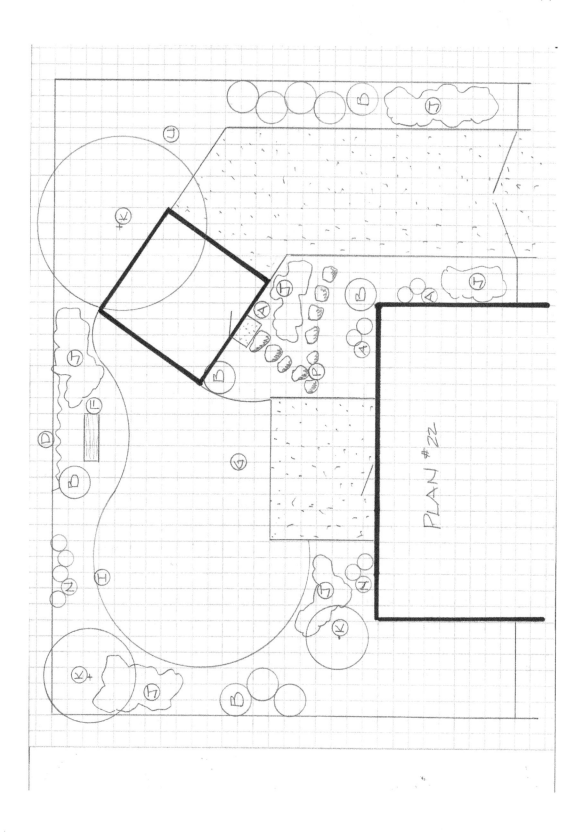

7

In Conclusion

Congratulations! You've done it!

You've done what you set out to do and created a custom landscape design using professional guidelines. The next step is to do a plant and material "take off" and create the materials list needed for the installation. Don't buy all your materials at one time. Buy what you need, as you need it, so that you don't run into the problem of having materials delivered all at once, only to find later that they're in the your way.

If you're not going to tackle the hardscape portion yourself, this is when you start making copies of your plan and putting it out for bids. The drainage and the hardscape are installed first. Ask the contractors that will be bidding on your project if they see any technical problems with your hardscape design like blocked drainage or encroachment into easements.

When you start buying plants, see if the retailer will give you a quantity discount if you pay for all the plants up front. I suggest that you buy from an independent nursery, they'll be of great help with your project. Use the phrase, "I want to buy all my plants for the project from you but I wanted to know if your designer could take a quick look at my design first." This will encourage the independent nurseryman to help you and correct any possible mistakes on our plan. Avoid the box stores, they are not likely have a designer that can help you, and the real pros usually work for the independent nurseries. Good luck with your project!

Keep an eye out for my next book on the installation phase. It's been a pleasure to help you and if you live in the Albuquerque, NM area and need help with your installation, call me for a bid. There's local information on landscaping in northern New Mexico at www.highdesertgardensinc.com

Happy Gardening!

Mike Dooley, Owner/Designer

Dooley Landscape Designs

CPSIA information can be obtained at www.ICGtesting.com
Printed in the USA
BVOW10s0008300514

354751BV00006B/128/P